DIVORCE RECOVERY

Raw, Real & Resilient

Paul F. Davis

INTRODUCTION

Resilience is the ability to bounce back, spring forth (like nature breaking through the dead of winter), rebound, stretch forth into new life, and return to your previous position and the Creator's original intent.

Recovering from a devastating setback, heartbreak, painful relationship that once brought you joy and fulfillment, but now brings you heartache, adversity and quite possibly depression, is no easy task. The emotional rollercoaster can take you all over the map from feelings of deep depression giving birth to suicidal thoughts to intense anger and hatred, giving you thoughts of murder and revenge. Thankfully, God and His Word are an anchor and steering wheel to reposition you in purity, ground you in emotional stability, and renew your mind in Christ Jesus the author and finisher of our faith (Hebrews 12:2), when we have nothing but a seed of hope and a willingness to walk by faith and not by sight.

Sometimes a drop of willingness to trust God and go forward despite the depths of your pain and anguish is all you have got, but my friend as someone who has survived two bad divorces, I can honestly and truthfully tell you, childlike faith in God and daily trust as you walk by faith not by sight is all you need to sustain you daily and to lift you up again to where you belong (in the heavenly Father's wonderful arms of love and warm embrace).

Failure is not final, but merely feedback and instruction as to how we can be better, improve and learn from our mistakes. Failing alone is tough, but failing in a relationship, especially a marriage that usually was publicly known and shown before all, is even more difficult and tumultuous. When you fail alone, not everyone sees it, knows, or cares. Yet when you fail at marriage, many people are involved, especially the near and dear family and friends of the person you were married to for however long.

This means people typically take sides. Usually the family and friends you had before marriage take your side (or her side if they were connected to her). A few wise, sincere souls actually hope for reconciliation and healing for both of you and take the high ground to love and pray for everyone involved (the husband, wife and any children effected).

Nevertheless, the truth is love and marriage are always evolving, maturing and a discovery process. Not everyone is willing to be flexible, love unconditionally and support their spouse through the many changes of life. In fact, controlling types (as was my 2nd ex-wife) may try to remake their spouse into their image and likeness to pursue their passions, purposes and preferences (which makes them happy, but their spouse miserable).

Realizing you are in a relationship with a control freak takes time to awake, see it clearly, and discern the person who you interacting with. Because often early on in a relationship, people hide the negative aspects of their personality.

Like playing poker, they don't reveal what is in their hand, their true intentions, nor what they ultimately have planned for their future spouse.

Clever, controlling, narcissistic and devious people rarely reveal their scheme and plan for the person they intend to prey on, manipulate and control after marriage. Only when the use and abuse reaches a breaking point and becomes unbearable in marriage do spouses begin contemplating divorce (and this usually after many heartfelt conversations, tearful prayers, and hours of counseling sessions).

Furthermore, narcissists often are unaware of their self-absorbed, narcissistic ways, nature and tendencies by which they control and dominate the loved ones in their lives to get their way and bulldoze everyone in their path. If you are in a relationship with such a person, you need to be discerning, proactive and protect yourself lest they suck every drop of life out of you and leave you lifeless within.

Some of my other books may prove helpful to you, depending on where you are in your personal development, life journey and relationships.

~ Daddy Loves Me

~ https://www.amazon.com/dp/B09SV688WY

~ Happiness Is An Inside Job

~ https://www.amazon.com/dp/B09WQDW41S

~ Angry at God & Everyone?

~ https://www.amazon.com/dp/1980911924

~ Oil For The Tin Man: Awaking The Heart

~ https://www.amazon.com/dp/1096848961

~ Update Your Identity: Transcend Labels to Live

~ https://www.amazon.com/dp/1521450455

~ Breakthrough For A Broken Heart

~ https://www.amazon.com/dp/1726786412

~ Step-Kids God's Kids

~ https://www.amazon.com/dp/1982904216

~ Are You Ready For True Love?

~ https://www.amazon.com/dp/B001A46ZJU

~ Men, Motives, Money & Marriage

~ https://www.amazon.com/dp/B09XLFHKDV

~ Dating, Relationships, Love & Marriage

~ https://www.amazon.com/dp/152092965X

~ Stop Lusting & Start Living

~ https://www.amazon.com/dp/B06XW35S2L

~ Adultery 101 Reasons Not to Cheat

https://www.amazon.com/dp/B001A6EK5O

~ Divorce Your Devil, Save Yourself & Marriage

~ https://www.amazon.com/dp/B07GMTCVBQ

~ Almighty Matchmaker: Dating & Relationships

~ https://www.amazon.com/dp/B01GZ8765M

1. LOVE

As a former lifeguard I know the power of a buoyant life-preserver, flotation device and life-saving plan prior to being in a life-threatening precarious predicament. As much as prenuptial agreements get a bad rap (and I've never used one thus far, but probably should have), they actually make couples think through turbulent times when sailing the sea of matrimony BEFORE they occur.

If lifeguards and emergency medical technicians can prepare beforehand for dangerous life-threatening situations before they occur in order to plan how they will assist the injured in pain who without their assistance otherwise may die; why can't couples also exercise the same humility and prudence to think through the many complications of life and undesirable scenarios that potentially could destroy their marriage and family?

The answer to that question is simply pride, denial and an unwillingness to talk about the uncomfortable realities of life (when the romance and passion of love feels so good and we want to prolong it as long as possible… and believe it will never end). Dating, romance, sex and the joys of love are great. Merge love and life together however and everything gets complicated and challenging, because dating and romance rarely is concerned with paying bills, taking out trash, doing dishes, washing laundry, changing diapers, getting the kids to school on time, and managing the many complexities of daily life when people live together.

Perhaps a prenuptial agreement can be a step in the right direction to sober up couples to talk about the complicated and challenging aspects of life, which are waiting for them after the wedding ceremony, celebratory reception and honeymoon. As painful as discussing these topics may be, actually doing so may be a step in the right direction to keep couples together, marriages intact and unify families.

Even if a prenuptial agreement is not signed, a written plan and agreement to deal with the daily complexities of life (how to live together harmoniously, what duties will be given to whom and how they will be equally divided, future plans for child bearing and caring, and a plan for retiring and aging) is something few couples "in love" do. Yet the longer these adult and important conversations are delayed, the harder they are to identify and discuss.

Undoubtedly, if we fail to plan, we plan to fail. Therefore, the sooner couples can have adult conversations (not just about sex, but about the daily complexities of life and their plan to successfully tackle them and work together harmoniously and equitably), the more likely they are to dwell together happily, live a life of victory, raise a peaceful family and ensure their loving union has longevity.

Likewise, a plan for dealing with temptation, the advances of outsiders seeking to seduce us or our spouse, and a strategy to affair proof our marriages is a wise move and vital discussion few couples have and therefore infidelity occurs when we least expect it, causing marriages to unravel and come undone.

The lie and illusion that love is only romance, passion and cannot behave with intelligence and a prudent plan beforehand must be discarded and a more proactive approach to marital bliss and long-term success pursued. Preparation and prudence is like a lifeguard's lifesaver (ready, waiting and nearby when needed), which can protect and preserve many marriages. Therefore, I encourage couples to have adult conversations about money, career goals, child bearing, where they want to live, dreams for the future, plans and purposes, how they define fulfillment and non-negotiables they are not willing to compromise on BEFORE they get married (so if they stay together, they can dwell together with knowledge).

Dwelling together with knowledge (1Peter 3:7) means you truly know the person you are living and building a life with; not just knowing them physically and sexually, but inwardly as to their thoughts, gifts, talents, abilities, goals, dreams and future plans for cultivating happiness and success.

God has much in His Word to say about prudence (thinking ahead beforehand), wisdom, knowledge and discretion. "I, wisdom, dwell together with prudence; I possess knowledge and discretion" (Proverbs 8:12).

Husbands are instructed to dwell with their wives using knowledge (1Peter 3:7). In other words, be knowledgeable about the person you are living with, or intending to marry and living with for the rest of your life. The more you know about a person, the more you can collaborate, cooperate and work together harmoniously to fulfill your goals and dreams. In fact, without knowledge, going forth blindly together can even cause your prayers to be hindered God says in His Word (1Peter 3:7). Therefore, couples must have adult conversations and talk through tough topics to truly know how one another thinks and will act in certain situations.

Jesus said, "From the abundance of the heart, the mouth speaks" (Matthew 12:34). Therefore, getting your special someone to talk will reveal what is truly inside of them, how they think, and the extent to which they are compatible (or not compatible) with you.

People who think differently and are not in agreement have no business getting married, lest they bring a world of torment upon one another. The Bible clearly tells us people who are not in agreement cannot walk together (Amos 3:3). Yet many times people override what they know to be true merely to marry someone who is good looking outwardly, but have nothing in common with them inwardly. However, they make for a nice photo on social media and the person with them feels important because they married someone easy on the eyes.

Nevertheless, someone easy on the eyes is rarely easy on the ears. Although my 2nd wife was a former Canadian model, I quickly learned she loved her fashion blog and social media photos more than me her husband. It turned out to be a 10 year sexless marriage (and she rarely cooked). Think about that for a while before you marry someone simply based on appearances.

It is better to be with someone with whom you have a genuine connection and not just a physical attraction. If the connection is not there, it will be difficult to sustain the relationship and/or marriage. Many men have left beautiful wives to be with average looking women who understand and can relate to them, Prince Charles of England being one of them.

Love therefore must be examined and evaluated from a spiritual, mental and physical capacity; not merely physically to the neglect of the spiritual and mental arena. Compatibility and connection occurs and is sustained in all three arenas. Neglecting any of these can prove to be destructive when your spouse seeks such a connection with someone else (when you fail to connect on this level).

Cultivating your own personal development, enrichment, purpose and fulfillment makes you more solid, complete, content, happy and attractive to another person in a relationship. Otherwise you will be an unfulfilled bottomless pit overly leaning and

relying on someone else to make you happy

(as did my 2nd ex-wife who was a drama

queen, always having to be the center of

attention). I never knew what a "drama queen"

was until I surprisingly married one and

discovered this after we were living together.

Such discoveries are best made before

you marry someone, not afterward. Therefore, I

urge people to slow down and take their time

when getting to know someone. Do not fear

losing someone. If you can lose them, they

were never yours to begin with. It's the person

who remains by your side for years steadfast,

unshakeable, immoveable and always faithful

through the thick and thin seasons of life that

you want to marry (not a fair weather friend

with good looks who only comes around during the good times, romantic dates and expensive getaway trips).

Hindsight is always 20/20 and pain is a great teacher, though quite costly and burdensome. Nevertheless, as you let God Almighty, our beloved heavenly Father, be your lifesaver and flotation device, you can supernaturally rise above your turbulent troubles and painful past as you position your heart and mind in childlike faith to trust the loving, living God to lead, guide, uphold and keep you my friend.

Keep your head up. The sun always shines above the clouds and our God is always several steps ahead of the devil seeking to destroy you. God Almighty can redeem your life from destruction, redirect your paths, order your steps and stops, calm the chaos and confusion caused by your ignorance and past mistakes (along with silence the noise of your enemies so your soul can rest in peace and recover to go forward into your personal promised land with new vision, hope and direction).

God is faithful and will surely show Himself strong on your behalf when your heart is repentant, pure through the blood of Christ, prayerful, steadfast, sensitive to the Holy Spirit, humble, flexible, pliable and willing to follow the leading of the Lord into the new life and blessings God has prepared for you.

1. LOVE

Love is a word so often misappropriated, misused, abused and misaligned with things nothing of the sort. People "love" their favorite peanut butter, coffee, car, TV show, clothing manufacturer and parent (until they disagree with and try to discipline them). Kids "love" their parents until it's time for discipline and punishment. Teenagers dating "love" one another, until they reach their first disagreement, have a fight, and breakup. Married couples "love" one another, until financial stress, strain and bill collectors arrive to repossess their car and house (when they fall upon tough times economically and lose their jobs).

The Greeks have at least three words for love. Eros speaks of erotic, romantic love. Phileo speaks of brotherly love (where the name for the city of Philadelphia comes from). Agape speaks of the unconditional God kind of love, which is precisely what parents have for their selfish, rude, unkind and disobedient children who take them for granted for 18 or more years, until they move out of their parents' home to secure their own place and professional career to provide for themselves.

Agape, the God kind of love, is unconditional, enduring and persevering through hard times and does not easily throw in the towel and quit just because it becomes uncomfortable to remain faithful, kind and committed to a person suffering through various life challenges.

Suffering is part of survival and most definitely a level of love few younger people know. Parents and grandparents know suffering quite well, especially suffering in relationships with their spouses and children. The reality is kids don't always treat their parents well.

At some point in their growth, when kids reach a certain age, they suddenly think they know it all, become a bit arrogant, rude, disrespectful, get an attitude and are not as loving and kind to their parents as they used to be when they were younger. It is a very painful, disheartening season in the parent-child relationship for the parent. Sometimes teenagers don't even want to walk alongside their parents in a shopping mall, lest they not appear cool.

Rest assured however when it comes time to pay for their new school clothes at the beginning of the academic year, the teenager is more than happy to stand alongside their parent and have them pay. This is just a small taste of what it feels like to be a mistreated, disrespected, belittled and discounted parent after you have given birth and your entire life to invest in and raise your child.

Long before the child is truly an adult and self-sufficient they enter a season of life, while still living under mom and dad's roof, that they think they are so cool and no longer need to respect and listen to their parents. Many parents would love to open the door and tell their rude, disrespectful kids to leave during this season. Yet the majority of parents smile and endure it, while continuing to provide for their child and loving them unconditionally.

The same level of sacrifice often applies in marriage when a spouse reaches a time when they take you for granted, expect you to do things for them, which they no longer say "thank you" for. Sometimes a spouse, like a teenager, reaches a point that they think they are smarter and cooler than you, begin to discount, belittle and disrespect you.

Yet, like my grandparents and parents, many couples stay together despite these toxic attitudes and strains in their relationship. That is what you call unconditional love, suffering and making a sacrifice to stay together. It's not roses, butterflies, romantic and beautiful; but such a commitment and willingness to suffer and endure one another is part of sustaining a marriage and survival. Of course, in a perfect world, a marriage would never have to endure such belittling and disrespectful attitudes, because partners would always love, uphold and esteem one another. Unfortunately, however many of us do not appreciate people until they have left our lives and we wake up and realize what a blessing they were to us.

I urge you therefore to remain sensitive, appreciate, kindhearted, tenderhearted, thankful, polite and respectful toward people (rather than taking them for granted due to familiarity, which can breed contempt and disdain). Maintain a humility of heart and mind. It will sustain your relationships and ensure you don't have to live alone to come to a place of self-awareness.

The best place to begin after having endured a painful divorce is to forgive yourself and your ex (husband or wife). Arguably, you were younger and dumber when you met and first started dating. Now you know more about yourself and them, whereby you felt it was wise to divorce and move on. Trust your instincts and understanding of issues pertaining to compatibility, happiness and your ability to cooperate harmoniously to remain together.

Forgive your ex for their past failures, along with the hurt and pain they caused you (plus the hurt and pain you caused them). I recommend writing a letter apologizing for your past wrongs committed that hurt them to cleanse your soul, heart and mind. Thereafter you can shut the door on the past, forgive yourself and them to move on and begin anew. You however cannot have a new beginning until you first have an old ending, finish well by being honest to yourself and others who you shared your life with. Some soul cleansing (like annual spring cleaning of the home) is healthy and will renew you to see with a clean heart and clear eyes.

2. SACRIFICE

Sacrifice in Judaic culture is something Jewish priests do to make an atonement for the sins of people. The offering of animal, plant, or human life (or of some material possession) to God, is a form of propitiation, substitution, or homage. In a relationship, giving yourself for someone else's happiness can be evident in many ways.

Listening to someone talk about a topic you have no interest in is a small sacrifice many of us do because we love someone. Driving your kids to athletic practice and watching them play a sport we may not find particularly fascinating is another form of sacrifice and an act of love. Going with your wife to a shopping mall to pick out new sheets, curtains or furniture may not be a man's dream, but he does it to make his wife happy. Likewise, a wife accompanying her husband to a ballgame or boxing match, may not do anything to stimulate and excite her in the slightest. Yet she may do it to make her man happy and be supportive. Multiply such experiences over the course of 20 to 50 years and you soon see what sacrifice looks like over one's lifetime.

Therefore, it is in your best interest to marry someone with whom you have something in common, lest you be dragged along to do things with them you do not care about and have no interest in for years of your life. Nevertheless, even if you find a woman (or man) with whom you have several mutual interests, there still will be areas you have no mutual interest and you will likely get dragged along and need to make some sacrifices anyhow.

Saying no all of the time and being a loner does not make for a good relational connection nor marriage. Take it from a man who has been divorced twice and knows how to say no without feeling guilty. Maintaining a strong relational connection will cost you something by way of your time and personal interests.

Prepare for that sacrifice and know it before entering into marriage.

Marriage is murder, meaning it will kill you in many parts of your life and require you to lay your life on the altar to make another person happy. Such self-sacrifice is something the older generation knows very well, but rarely talks about. They should talk about it so the younger generation could be more emotionally intelligent when it comes to relationships and marriage. Otherwise couples enter marriage thinking it is all about sex and making babies. The reality however is marriage is murder, killing your ego, sacrificing yourself, giving yourself to make someone else happy and then exponentially and repeatedly dying to self again as you bring forth children into your family. Nevertheless, with every death there is a corresponding resurrection and joy that follows (the miracle of life, newborns, children and family).

To what extent are you ready to surrender, permit injury, be disadvantaged, discounted, take the backseat for someone else, eat dinner at someone else's favorite restaurant, spend time outside of your comfort zone to make someone else happy, and offer yourself up continually to ensure, sustain and feed someone else's happiness? This my friend is sacrifice.

The more of yourself you give, the more meaningful of a relationship you will get (although at first it doesn't always feel like it and seems a bit like suicide as you increasingly die to yourself).

3. SELF-AWARENESS

Although I may not be the most sacrificial kind of guy when it comes to doing things to make my spouse happy, when it comes to children, I give more of myself happily. The more self-aware you are, the more you can try to find a person who understands and is willing to do life with you on your terms.

It however will take many conversations as you reveal yourself and get to know one another. Usually every relationship has a person who is more giving of themselves and sacrificial. I would call this the bigger person in the relationship and perhaps the one who empowers the other person to fulfill their purpose.

Ideally, it is preferred for both people to have the liberty, freedom and support they need to pursue and fulfill their dreams. Yet when you bring kids into the picture and family, someone will need to attend to their needs (preferably both of you) and make additional sacrifices to do so.

If you marry a medical doctor, lawyer, or pastor; expect added sacrifices by reason of their profession. If you do not like going to church regularly (and perhaps daily), do not marry a pastor (or priest). If you hate hospitals and conversations about sick patients, do not marry a doctor or nurse. If the law is of little interest to you and conversations about trials in court bore you, do yourself a favor and do not marry a lawyer.

Unfortunately, many people don't think like this when they are dating. On the contrary, they say to themselves, "Wow. He is a lawyer and must make a lot of money. He is also good looking. I should marry him." Then once they are married, she hates that he is so argumentative and always talking about the law and court cases.

Self-awareness however will give you a reality check and enable you to be more brutally honest and truthful with yourself and those you are dating (and considering marrying). Self-awareness begins with humility as you increasingly come to terms with knowing yourself (the good, bad and ugly).

The more you know and can share these things about yourself with people desirous of being a part of your life (to forewarn and prepare them), the more likely you are to find someone who is compatible with you and capable of living alongside you and loving you unconditionally. Not telling and revealing these aspects of your life and nature to others however can be deceptive and deluding, because once they are living with you and discover them, they may suddenly pull back and not know what to do with you.

It is therefore wise to be truthful, up front and honest early on about your disposition, lifestyle, mannerisms, ways, tendencies, peculiarities, challenging difficulties and proclivities to ensure people who enter a relationship with you do so with both eyes wide open and know full well what they are signing up for. This will increase your relational understanding for one another and substantially increase your likelihood of relational success.

4. DISCOVERY

Life is a discovery process. If you are

young, or relatively young (30 years of age or

less) you still likely have a lot to learn about

yourself, career, passions, purpose and lifelong

dreams. We all evolve, mature, grow, develop

over time, and discover new interests and

facets about our character and human nature.

I personally feel when a person connects

with God their Creator and their spirit is

awakened (Romans 8:16; Ephesians 1:17-19),

a whole new realm of self-discovery breaks

forth to illuminate their path and shine the light

on their gifts, talents and abilities. Moreover,

once the Spirit of God has been

acknowledged, welcomed and is moving in, on

and through your life; the supernatural begins

to occur to advance your inner and professional growth at an accelerated rate.

Some of the books I have written about this are:

Supernatural Fire: Unquenchable & Unstoppable

~ https://www.amazon.com/dp/B07K3T9KYC

Success Principles ~ https://www.amazon.com/Success-Principles-Purpose-Prosperity-Happiness-ebook/dp/B08SLLSPG4

Wealthy Mind

~ https://www.amazon.com/dp/1982955732

Creativity ~ https://www.amazon.com/CREATIVITY-Transcend-Transform-Paul-

As you grow, mature and evolve some people will feel they have lost the ability to relate with you. Not so, it's just that you have grown and added new depths, layers and realms of relatability; some of which they know nothing about and cannot relate to (where they currently are spiritually). Nevertheless, you can still connect based on your past experiences, friendships and understanding. However, as you go deeper in God and further in your journey of discovery (in life, pertaining to your purpose, the level on which you relate to others, understand yourself, and what matters most to you) your values may have a significant and substantial shift to bring about an inner realignment and repositioning to set you up for your destiny and thereby adjust your own sense of certainty and identity.

Thereafter some may think you are arrogant as a result of you being confident. Others may accuse you of self-importance when you discover how important you are to God and your divine purpose. Do not let the insecurity of others derail your destiny, dwarf your potential and who God created you to be. Express yourself freely and live wholeheartedly. Do not hold back who you are to make someone else feel comfortable.

Let your friendships naturally evolve (as you do) and if necessary realign and change (should you wish to connect with others more in agreement with who you presently are and where you are going in your life by way of your divine purpose). Those discoveries and decisions are yours to make. Be patient through the process and if necessary be willing to walk alone for a time until God brings people into your life who understand the new you as the transformation takes place, unfolds and you evolve.

Remember you do not need to explain yourself. Just give yourself liberty to be free to be and gradually reveal yourself to those desirous of interacting and being with you. Over time people will decide if you are the kind of person they want to be with and let it be however those associations and relationships unfold (assuming you feel the same and want to be with them).

Friendships and relationships can simply be pure, not physical, based on a similar interest, occupation, purposeful pursuit, genuine intent or initiative. People will come and go in your life. Joyfully and peacefully accept and embrace that as part of life. You cannot play God and control people. Embrace and welcome the adventure and let your heart take you wherever the Spirit of God woos, draws, leads and guides you (John 3:8).

Don't be fearful or in a hurry, trying to force things that are not ready, nor in place for you. Purpose, people, places and positioning takes time (Ecclesiastes 3:11). Let God work His miracles and bring all of these into proper alignment, synergy and synchronicity. Let the supernatural happen naturally and as it progressively unfolds enjoy the journey. God has special miracles just for you (Acts 19:11).

Contact me for prayer (RevivingNations@yahoo.com), to schedule life coaching, prophetic ministry and/or college & career counseling depending on what season you are in and what you are presently pursuing in your life.

PropheticPowerShift.com

EducationPro.us

PaulFDavis.com

I speak around the world if you desire me to come minister in your city, church, local college and/or school.

5. COMPATABILITY

If and when a new friend, or love interest appears in your life; rejoice and take it happily and intentionally slow to fully discover all there is to know about them (and reveal yourself gradually to them as well). Do not be in a hurry. Do not be fearful, or desperate. Take your time and let things evolve and unfold naturally. Otherwise you rob yourself of the dating season, which itself is a lovely time in which people get to know one another and assess their compatibility.

Do not make swift decisions merely based on your emotional loneliness or physical desires to be with someone. Compatibility is a time consuming discovery process. If you don't like the person and they suddenly begin to annoy you, put on the breaks and stop the phone conversations, texts and in person interactions. You have no obligation to be in relationship with anyone. Ultimately, happiness is an inside job. If you cannot be happy alone, you will never be happy with anyone else.

Take it slow and proceed forward only to the extent a person brings joy and meaning into your life. When that stops, I recommend pulling back and not committing to a relationship that no longer brings you joy and life. Doing so merely out of obligation and guilt is a dangerous way to begin a relationship, which rarely can be sustained for long on those terms. Pursue healthy life-giving relationships, not those that weigh you down like a ball and chain, or sack of potatoes and make your heart heavy.

Wisdom, discernment and restraint will tell you when to put the brakes on a relationship before it becomes toxic, intrusive and violates you as a person. Pursue healthy relationships and run from toxic people who pollute and defile your soul, complicate your life, burden and trouble your heart. If you are married, those sacrifices are something you signed up for. However, if you are not married and feel inner warnings, see red flags popping up, and feel agitated within when with a person; listen to those divine inner impressions and warnings to save yourself a lot of heartache and spare yourself years of trouble. Do not go forward with a person if you see a train wreck ahead. Be wise and discerning. Listen to your gut and trust your instincts.

6. HONESTY

Brutal honesty with yourself and others early on can save you from a lot of relational, marital and lifelong hardship. It's when we lie to ourselves, override our conscience, quiet our spirit, ignore the whispers of God and the still small voice of the Holy Spirit that we enter into troublesome situations, harmful relationships and dangerous circumstances once we have covenanted with a person within a marital union. Thereafter it will take a long time to undo what has been done. Moreover, once children are brought into this world, such relationships become even more difficult and painful to unravel, disentangle, direct and protect their purity, your purpose and the family structure when marital disharmony and disintegration occur.

Do yourself a favor and take it slow early on within a relationship to truly get to know a person, see them interact with others, encounter difficult and challenging situations, leave their comfort zone geographically and culturally, watch them when things go wrong and they are annoyed, and behold how they respond when their buttons are pushed and things are not going their way. Watch how they treat insignificant people at restaurants, on the job, at hotels, and janitorial staff. How they treat the lowest level people will be how they will treat you when you live together.

It is through real life situations that the true person within, their character, nature and values are revealed. Until this person has been tested and observed under pressure in the above mentioned scenarios (and many more), you truly do not know someone. Prematurely jumping into a committed relationship and marital engagement before you know a person can be the worst thing you've ever done. I know by experience.

If you want to disrupt, detour, distract, dislocate and immobilize your lifelong progress; a bad marriage is the perfect recipe to do so and set your disaster in motion.

Honesty concerning your blind spots, character flaws, weaknesses, tendencies, peculiarities, preferences, bad habits, laziness, inabilities, strengths, skills (or lack thereof), weaknesses, ignorance, intelligence, biases and prejudices will help both you and those you date discern whether or not you are a good fit. Likewise, it is important to discuss non-negotiables or areas of inflexibility, such as where geographically you want to live, how many kids you want to have, when you desire to begin having children, holiday plans, people you will maintain connection with in your life, expectations for your future spouse, and every other imaginable question you can think of.

My first ex-wife assumed I would happily spend holidays with her family and be willing to pay the expenses to do so. Yet I was less than enthusiastic about spending time with her dysfunctional family, though they were all lovely and kind people. Her parents were divorced. Her mother lived in upstate New

York. Her sister lived in Chicago. Her brother

lived in Texas and her eldest sister lived in

Boston. I traveled with her to New York and

Chicago to see family and enjoyed doing so,

but to expect your future spouse to travel

across the nation or world to see your family

every year (when you are not contributing any

money toward the expenses of doing so is

unreasonable).

I had a similar experience with my 2nd ex-

wife who also expected me to travel to Canada

to see her mother and grandmother, plus take

her from Florida where we lived to see her

father in California. I did all of these and fully

paid for it myself. Yet my 2nd ex-wife was quite

the monster on the trip to Canada. In fact, I got

along better with her mother on vacation

traveling down the St. Lawrence River than my ex-wife. This was another sign and indicator I was not meant to be with my ex-wife, as she was miserable and complaining even on vacations (including in Paris, Greece, a Caribbean cruise, a beach in Florida and Disney World). Even her mother was appalled and concerned with my ex-wife's behavior.

If the person you are with cannot have fun and be happy on vacation, this is a pretty good indication you may not want to spend your life with them. Nevertheless, I was already married by this time and was committed. Therefore, I endured such nonsense for 10 years, until thankfully she secretly moved to California to be near her father and filed for separation in route to divorce.

In fact, the last 2 and ½ years of my second marriage, I was sleeping on the couch in the living room because my ex would wake me up all of the time in the middle of the night to tell me I was snoring, or would talk nonstop during bedtime (sometimes until 1:30am). This ten-year long sexless marriage was full of words, nonstop chatter, endless complaints, defiance, manipulation, verbal abuse, attempts to control me and pity parties when I refused to be controlled.

A Filipina I dated years after my divorce, told me I actually do not snore and refuted the complaints of my ex concerning me. It just goes to show you, if a person wants to be a troublemaker, there are endless things they can create, say and do to cause you trouble and make your life miserable. Be wise as to who you allow to have access into your life and make sure their heart is pure lest they pollute you and drive you crazy day and night.

The first two years of my 2nd marriage when the intense manipulation and attempts to control me began, I told my wife: "You can love me, or leave me. I am not changing." Thankfully, after 10 years she realized what I said was true and she finally left. I only cried for my daughter when my ex-wife left, as sadly I had not felt any love in the marriage for a very long time.

The stupid things we do and endure for love (plus pride, ego and vanity), even to the extent of subjecting ourselves to such pain and emotional trauma. The two emotions I often felt were anger and depression. I got to the point I began praying: "God change her, or please remove her from my life. I can't do this anymore." Thankfully, God eventually answered that prayer.

Apart we are now much more happy. After having divorced 6 years ago, she is now happily engaged living with her boyfriend (and my daughter) in Colorado. I am in California enjoying my freedom, traveling often with my daughter internationally and across the nation on holidays (not having to be bullied or answer to anyone telling me how to live my life, or where to live geographically).

As for my first ex-wife, she had an affair with a Muslim guy. When she told me (upon picking me up at the airport following a ministry trip I did to Africa), I reclined the seat of the car and just kept quiet. After I consulted Bishop Bill Hamon as to what I should do, he advised me to let her make her decisions first and thereafter I could decide which direction I would go.

In my spirit, I kept hearing God telling me, "No more mercy. Judgment has come." I fought it and didn't want to divorce her. In fact, I gave her breakfast in bed for 2 weeks and tried to reconcile. Yet she often continued coming home late at night, once at 2am she returned a bit drunk and claimed to have been out with "friends" (who I suspected were men).

When I made the decision to proceed to file for divorce, upon filing the divorce papers in Seminole County, Florida and leaving the government building; on the courthouse steps I heard the Spirit of God say to me: "Well done good and faithful servant."

I was shocked and said to the Lord, "God, your Word says you hate divorce (Malachi 2:16). How can I be good after filing for divorce?"

The Spirit of God replied, "Because I hate the lukewarm and I spit them out of my mouth" (Revelation 3:16).

It was then I realized God has compassion on we who are struggling, sinking, suffering, miserable and dying within while being married. I have never felt such death as being in a lifeless and loveless marriage.

In fact, there is a documentary channel that has many forensics and law shows I watched for months in the San Francisco Bay area when I lived there. To my surprise many of the *Sex & Murder* forensic shows actually traced the murderer (or attempted murderer) to be a husband or wife. Often spouses killed their husbands or wives to collect insurance money, reclaim their freedom, or to get rid of their spouse so they could date someone else.

Often these murderers even had children with the spouse they killed (or tried to kill). It was then I realized compared to murder, divorce was not so bad after all. At least one Christian man killed his wife, because he knew the Bible said divorce was immoral. Yet I guess he forgot the 10 commandments, which state you shall not kill (Exodus 20).

The Bible permits divorce in the case of adultery and marital unfaithfulness (Matthew 5:32). The apostle Paul also spoke of allowing the unbelieving spouse to depart (1Corinthians 7:15) and the other spouse thereafter not being under bondage, since God desires peace for people more than marital strife and heartache.

As distasteful, undesirable, painful and dreadful as divorce is; after having experienced how miserable being married to someone who is unhappy and complaining endlessly can be, I now appreciate the option of divorce and consider it a better alternative than lifelong misery or murder. It is appalling and shocking to see how many people actually attempt to kill their spouse to get rid of them. Thank God I never contemplated or tried such a thing, as we both love our daughter and remained together for her.

However, parents fighting and bickering in disagreement constantly is not good for children either. Therefore, I am thankful we found a way to move on despite the gut wrenching tragedy of losing my daughter in the process.

I pray for a better way for everyone with children, but preserving the wellbeing of the parents is also in the interest of children. As I learned when I was a lifeguard, you have to protect yourself first, lest you be useless and no good to anyone else needing your assistance.

7. DECISIONS

I have made the decision to go where I am celebrated not merely where I am tolerated. This applies to work and jobs I take, as well as relationships I enter into. I cannot be with a halfhearted, miserable and antagonistic person.

Do yourself a favor and run from toxic people lest they contaminate you. Of course if you are presently married, pray together and seek marital counseling (even better counseling for the individual alone so they can get help and heal). Sometimes people need inner healing and to resolve their own unfinished business before they bring their bitterness and wounds into a new relationship only to perpetuate their pain with new people in a different place.

You cannot run from your past pain. You must get healed, receive the forgiveness of God, let the cross of Christ position you to forgive, crossover and live anew. The blood of the cross of Christ can reconcile your relationships, heal your heart, resolve your past, close the door on past pains, position you for new life and greatness, and propel you forward.

Go to God in prayer. Get on your knees and humbly cry out to God to heal you within, remove the roots of bitterness, heal your wounds, wash away your pain and renew you afresh in Jesus Name.

Thereafter when you get off your knees, forget the past. Go forward without apology. Release those who have hurt you and stop renting space to them in your heart and mind.

Rid your soul of their memory to go forward with childlike faith and renewed hope. Arise with a renewed sense of purpose, a fresh purity and understanding of the goodness of God Almighty, and stop talking about your past relationship(s) with people, lest they pull your heart and mind backward and hinder your forward progress.

Go forward boldly without apology. I wrote my books to close the door on the past, while helping people simultaneously struggling in similar situations. Anyone needing inner healing, breakthrough and to divorce their devil can read my books to find help, wisdom, encouragement and empowerment to do so.

BREAKTHROUGH FOR A BROKEN HEART

~ https://www.amazon.com/dp/1726786412

DIVORCE YOUR DEVIL -

~ https://www.amazon.com/dp/B07GMTCVBQ

May God bless you with heavenly vision,
newness of life and peace that surpasses
understanding to end all conflict and strife. Let
Jesus Christ crucify your past and lovingly lift
you up to where you belong, so you can see
with fresh vision and perspective to enter into
your personal promised land with childlike faith,
anticipation, expectation and joyful boldness.

8. FORGETTING THE PAST

None of us have fully apprehended that for which God has called us. If we had, or if we had even fully tried and completed our journey on earth; we would be dead and no more. Because when God is done with a person, He lets him enjoy the remainder of his life and afterward takes him home to heaven.

If we are alive, we have a purpose and destiny to pursue in God. To fulfill our purpose, we have to first forget our past and behold a vision of our future. You cannot follow after your future while looking through the rearview mirror with regret in your soul. Let the past go. Forget it and boldly move forward with happiness and a wholehearted earnest expectation for good things ahead of you.

The apostle Paul lived by this principal, always forgetting the past (even his past successes and accomplishments, lest they distract and derail his future). We too must press toward the mark for the prize of the high calling of God in Christ Jesus and forget the past to be free inwardly to pursue the greatness that God has for us and step into our future (see Philippians 3:13-14).

9. GOING FORWARD

Going forward requires reckless abandonment and throwing caution to the wind. Otherwise if you are bound to a memory, you are kept in a straightjacket and unable to freely pursue your future.

When my 2nd ex-wife kidnapped my daughter and stole my car without telling me (while I was in Indonesia for a week exploring a job opportunity) and moved to California; I returned an empty home in Orlando, Florida with no daughter, no car, less furniture and a couple of days thereafter a guy pounding on my door to deliver a legal document stating my ex-wife was filing for legal separation in route to divorce.

Rather than sit at home and cry, I immediately fought back, filed for divorce with an excellent female attorney, after which by law my ex had to return my daughter to Florida and negotiate an agreeable divorce settlement and parental arrangement. Yet while fighting back, I had to walk and ride a bicycle through the Florida summer heat, humidity and rain. Nevertheless, while doing so, I victoriously praised and worshipped God on my bicycle and prayed fervently for breakthroughs and blessings.

God did not disappoint me and did great things on my behalf, increasing me financially and gave me the book "*Divorce Your Devil*" as I went through the painful circumstances to thereby help and strengthen others around the world.

God is always up to something good. You just have to remember the loving nature of God, be mindful of His goodness, expect, look for and pursue it. Trust and obey whatever the Holy Spirit births in your heart and shows you to do. Boldly do so with childlike faith, doubting nothing, and as you put feet to your faith God will not disappoint you.

God Almighty has taken me to 90 nations of the world and sustained me every step of the way. Sometimes I traveled to nations with less than $50 in my pocket and no guarantee anything solid waited for me upon arrival (as was the case when I took my first teaching job in mainland China).

Walking by faith not by sight can be challenging, but going nowhere because of your unbelief and being stuck stagnating is far worse and much more painful. Therefore, I encourage you to trust God, take chances and make advances.

God will surely not disappoint you, but will hold your hand each and every step of the way, ordering your steps, stops, setting up divine relationships and orchestrating divine appointments to bless you beyond your wildest dreams. According to your faith, be it unto you my friend (Matthew 9:29).

Pray fervently, obey boldly and throw caution to the wind as you expectantly trust God and believe for great things from the living, loving Lord God Almighty. He will not disappoint you, as you release and relinquish control, allow Him

to show Himself strong, and lead and guide you

all day long.

10. VISION FOR THE FUTURE

Get yourself a journal and write down what God says to you daily during your prayer and meditation time. It is during those times of stillness, peace and quiet that the Holy Spirit whispers within you, drops divine ideas in your spirit, shows you visions and divine insights, illuminates your path and way forward, and inspires you which way to go. The more you pray and practice the Presence of God throughout your day, remembering that God by the Holy Spirit is with and in you, always ready to lead and guide you; it is then the Lord of light and life will illuminate your path forward and show you which way to go, how to do things with excellence and give you victory in all of your endeavors (as you yield to

His guidance and give Him the glory for every victory).

"Where there is no vision, people perish" (Proverbs 29:18). Plant your life in a strong Bible believing church, where you can fervently worship the living God, dwell in a life-giving spiritual atmosphere, grow in a vibrant community and family of faith, hear the Word of God preached with prophetic conviction and thereby grasp for your life God's heavenly vision.

The apostle Paul was not disobedient to the heavenly vision he received from God (Acts 26:19). Moses had a blueprint from heaven, when God gave him a vision for how to build the tabernacle. Every man and woman needs to go to God in prayer, press through their flesh, transcend the carnal mind and bypass the arrogance of their top heavy brain to be enlightened with heavenly vision from above. The Spirit of the living God will breathe fresh vision in your spirit as you approach Him with humility, ask for divine wisdom, revelation and insight.

Draw near to God with hunger and humility, after which He will surely draw near to you and open your eyes to see clearly (James 4:8; Ephesians 1:17-19). The kingdom of God is preached, but every person must earnestly press into God for themselves (Luke 16:16). Do so and be greatly blessed. Your best and most blessed days are ahead of you. Trust the living God for new love, new life, new blessings, new doors of opportunity to open, new breakthroughs, new advances, new friendships, new relationships, new business and divine connections to accelerate your purpose and propel you into the promised land God has prepared for you.

Be encouraged my friend. God is trying to get good things to you. God has not forgotten you. Believe with childlike faith. Pray and put feet to your feet every day and watch the many miracles God will do for, in and through you as you partner with the living God.

Contact Paul for prophetic ministry, life coaching, college and career counseling, or to speak in your city.

PaulFDavis.com

EducationPro.us

PropheticPowerShift.com

Tinyurl.com/PaulFDavis-books

Tiktok.com/@RevivalForTheNations

RevivingNations@yahoo,com